1 MONTH OF
FREE
READING

at

www.ForgottenBooks.com

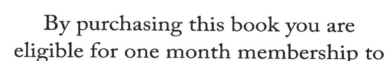

By purchasing this book you are
eligible for one month membership to
ForgottenBooks.com, giving you
unlimited access to our entire
collection of over 1,000,000 titles via
our web site and mobile apps.

To claim your free month visit:
www.forgottenbooks.com/free964073

ISBN 978-0-260-68359-5
PIBN 10964073

Forgotten Books is a registered trademark of FB &c Ltd.
Copyright © 2018 FB &c Ltd.
FB &c Ltd, Dalton House, 60 Windsor Avenue, London, SW19 2RR.
Company number 08720141. Registered in England and Wales.

For support please visit www.forgottenbooks.com

Historic, archived document

Do not assume content reflects current
scientific knowledge, policies, or practices.

Foreign Library

CROPS AND MARKETS

VOLUME 60   **NUMBER 17**

WORLD SHEEP NUMBERS   (Page 378)

U.S. Foreign Agricultural Trade   (Page 382)

CONTENTS

FOR RELEASE

MONDAY

APRIL 24, 1950

UNITED STATES DEPARTMENT OF AGRICULTURE
OFFICE OF FOREIGN AGRICULTURAL RELATIONS
WASHINGTON 25, D. C.

LATE NEWS

The Government of India had issued licenses for importation of 238,000 bales of cotton (194,000 bales of 500 pounds gross) by the middle of March and announced that additional licenses (quantities not mentioned) would be granted for importation of long-staple cotton (1-1/8 inches or longer) from the United States before the end of June 1950. Issuance of import licenses for United States cotton was previously discontinued after February 7, 1950, because applications on hand exceeded the import quota.

- - - - - -

The fourth official report placed the 1949-50 cotton crop in Pakistan at 957,000 bales (of 500 pounds gross) from 2,811,000 acres, compared with earlier estimates of 900,000 bales from 2,715,000 acres and revised estimates for 1948-49 of 832,000 bales from 2,799,000 acres. Higher yields per acre in 1949-50 are attributed to favorable weather and adequate water for irrigation. Production of American-type cotton rose from 707,000 bales in 1948-49 to 870,000 in 1949-50, while the crop of Asiatic types decreased from 125,000 to 87,000 bales.

- - - - - -

The 1949-50 cotton crop now being picked in the Union of South Africa is expected to reach a near record of 16,000 bales (of 500 pounds gross) from a planted area of 32,000 acres, compared with estimates of 4,000 bales and 8,000 acres in 1948-49. The sharp increase is attributed to higher prices stimulated by a rapidly expanding domestic spinning industry and to the recent development of a variety that is resistant to the jassid pest. Yields of about half a bale per acre were normal but heavier yields were in prospect until damage was sustained from drought and bollworm attack. All South African cotton has a staple length of 1-1/8 inch and longer according to South African standards. It is now selling at 2s 5d (U.S.$.34 cents) per pound.

FOREIGN CROPS AND MARKETS

Published weekly to inform producers, processors, distributors and consumers of farm products of current developments abroad in the crop and livestock industries, foreign trends in prices and consumption of farm products, and world agricultural trade. Circulation of this periodical is free to those needing the information it contains in farming, business and professional operations. Issued by the Office of Foreign Agricultural Relations of the U.S. Department of Agriculture, Washington 25, D.C.

WORLD SHEEP NUMBERS CONTINUE UPWARD TREND 1/

World sheep numbers at the beginning of 1950 are estimated at 730 million head in a preliminary report by the Office of Foreign Agricultural Relations. Although the trend continued upward, the overall gain in 1949 was relatively small and numbers were about 2 percent below the 1936-40 average. The very favorable grazing conditions during 1948 and 1949 and the continuance of high prices for wool, mutton and lamb encouraged sheep producers to expand their flocks, particularly in some of the major producing areas and in the war-devastated areas.

Sheep numbers throughout the world are likely to increase during 1950. The degree of such increase, however, will depend primarily on the continuance of the present relatively favorable grazing conditions. It is very probable that the price of wool in particular will continue high and the price of mutton and lamb may remain high in relation to prewar prices. Other factors that may have an impact on the sheep industry are the increasing population throughout most countries of the world and the increasing use of competitive or substitute products. Beyond 1950 the trend will be determined by the continuation of favorable price relationships for wool, mutton and lamb and the extent of competition from substitutes or competitive products.

The numbers at the beginning of 1950 in most of the sheep-producing countries either had increased or were maintained near their early 1949 level. The largest numerical gains, however, were in Australia, Algeria, the United Kingdom, the Soviet Union, French Morocco and India, and these increases more than offset the large declines that occurred in Argentina, Uruguay and Turkey and the smaller declines in the United States, Syria, and Germany. Notwithstanding the relatively high level of world sheep numbers, such important producing countries as the United States, the United Kingdom, Argentina, China, India, Pakistan, French Morocco, Algeria, Tunisia, and the Union of South Africa continue to be below and in some instances considerably under their 1936-40 levels.

In the United States and Canada, sheep numbers continued to decline, but last year's decreases were the smallest since the downward trend began. More profitable alternative farm enterprises during the postwar period and shortages of labor contributed largely to the downward trend. Argentina's drop in numbers may be attributed principally to competition of the cattle industry and the recent drought. Uruguayan sheep numbers, having reached a record level in 1949, can be expected to drop due to drought and overstocking which is resulting in heavy marketings.

The trend of European sheep numbers has been upward since 1945 and current estimates are about 10 percent below the 1936-40 average. Recovery of sheep numbers in the United Kingdom, one of the larger sheep-producing countries, was curtailed by heavy losses in the winter

---

1/ A more extensive statement may be obtained from the Office of Foreign Agricultural Relations, U. S. Department of Agriculture, Washington 25, D. C.

SHEEP: Number in specified countries, averages 1936-40 and 1941-45, annual 1945-1950

Continent and country	Month of estimate 1/	Average 1936-40 Thousands	Average 1941-45 Thousands	1945 Thousands	1946 Thousands	1947 Thousands	1948 Thousands	1949 2/ Thousands	1950 2/ Thousands
NORTH AMERICA									
Canada.............	Dec 1 1/	2,651:	2,710:	2,822:	2,456:	1,782:	1,587:	1,322:	1,235
Guatemala..........	July	273:1/	406:			1/	618:		
Mexico.............	Dec. 31 1/	4/5/4,809:1/	4,632:					5,100:	5,000
United States.....	Jan. 1	51,404:	52,517:	46,520:	42,436:	37,818:	34,827:	33,664:	30,197
Estimated total...		59,700:	60,800:	55,600:	51,300:	46,100:	42,800:	39,200:	38,200
EUROPE									
Albania............	Dec. 31 3/	1,576:		1,670:	1,700:				
Austria............	Dec. 31 3/	316:	400:	460:	391:	399:	474:	454:	375
Belgium............	Jan. 1 4/	187:	193:	199:	177:	144:	107:	155:	121
Bulgaria...........	Dec. 31 3/	8,746:	8,782:	7,100:	7,800:	8,784:			
Czechoslovakia.....	Jan. 1 3/	492:	511:	560:	510:	491:	386:	459:	480
Denmark............	July 15 4/	147:3/	198:	213:	170:	91:	77:	67:	
Eire...............	June	3,076:	2,681:	2,581:	2,423:	2,094:	2,058:	2,182:	
Finland............	Mar. 1 6/	1,007:	833:	1,015:	1,099:	982:	999:	1,067:	
France 7/..........	Fall	9,648:	7,162:	6,300:	6,632:	7,259:	7,406:	7,510:	7,325
Germany 8/.........	Dec. 31 1/13/	3,729:	4,050:		3,010:	3,000:	3,040:	3,220:	2,760
Greece.............	Dec. 31 3/	8,304:			6,262:	7,205:	7,056:	6,611:	6,656
Hungary............	Spring	1,490:	1,207:1/	328:1/	370:1/	488:1/	590:	650:	
Iceland............	Spring	624:	595:	532:	511:		505:1/	470:	
Italy..............	July 4/	9,350:	8,400:		8,600:	8,600:	9,190:	10,100:	
Netherlands........	May	656:	496:	489:	558:	460:	425:	464:	
Norway.............	June	1,742:	1,715:	1,760:	1,707:	1,698:	1,629:	1,8 810	
Poland.............	June 30 4/	1,941:	1/	710:1/	759:1/	983:	1,406:		
Portugal...........	Dec. 31 1/19/	3,948:	3,800:	3,500:	3,900:	4,000:	4,000:		
Rumania............	Dec. 31 1/3/	10,176:			6,799:	7,100:			
Spain..............	Dec. 31 1/4/	20,000:3/	23,509:	22,000:	20,183:			22,000:	
Sweden.............	Summer	398:	486:	516:	482:	421:	349:	313:	
Switzerland........	April 3/	177:	200:	192:	195:	182:	170:		
United Kingdom.....	June	26,112:	20,883:	20,150:	20,358:	16,713:	18,164:	19,493:	
Yugoslavia.........	Dec. 31 1/	9,796:							
Estimated total...		123,800:	113,100:	101,000:	101,700:	102,200:	106,200:	111,200:	112,500
U.S.S.R. (Europe and Asia)....	Jan. 1 4/	66,000:			61,100:	60,800:	64,800:	74,000:	78,000
ASIA									
Cyprus 10/.........	March	300:	303:	331:	315:	313:	291:		304
Iran...............	March 21	14,497:	13,854:	13,020:	12,950:	13,190:	13,200:	11,100:	10,900
Iraq...............	Jan. 1 3/	7,090:1/	6,719:	7,250:	8,000:	8,000:		9,100:	9,000
Syria..............	Dec. 31 1/3/	2,060:	2,539:	2,777:	3,091:	3,260:	3,176:	2,935:	2,443
Trans-Jordan.......		216:	293:	296:					
Turkey.............	Dec. 31 1/	21,656:	23,641:	22,450:	23,386:	23,528:	24,496:	25,500:	24,000
China 11/..........	May	26,000:	22,000:	21,000:	20,000:	22,000:			
India..............	Jan. 1 4/	41,000:4/	38,000:	38,000:					39,000
Indonesia..........	B. 31 1/13/	1,614:				1,610:			1,740
Pakistan...........	Jan. 1	8,000:4/	6,000:	6,100:			6,150:		6,500
Estimated total...		152,600:	145,300:	142,900:	144,300:	147,700:	148,200:	147,600:	146,200

Country	Date								
SOUTH AMERICA									
Argentina	July	44,900 3/	52,288 3/	56,182	55,000 12/	54,000	53,500	48,000	—
Bolivia	Dec. 31 1/	2,608 4/	3,987 3/	4,014	4,289	4,534	4,195	—	—
Brazil		11,438 3/	11,346	13,283	15,542	16,000	16,000	—	—
Chile	June	5,855 3/	6,057 3/	6,000	5,900	6,000	6,328	6,300	—
Colombia	Dec. 31 1/	916	1,240	1,168	—	1,013	1,013	1,061	—
Ecuador		—	1,400	1,443	—	—	1,802	—	1,200
Paraguay		159 3/	203 3/	210	255	—	—	252	—
Peru	Dec. 31 1/	14,900 3/	14,900	—	17,268	17,268	17,288	—	202
Uruguay	May	17,971 4/	20,289 4/	—	19,559	17,288 1/	22,000	25,000	—
Estimated total		100,900	113,700	120,100	121,100	122,300	123,500	120,600	115,400
AFRICA									
Algeria 10/	Nov. 1 1/	6,180	6,071	5,832	5,376	4,800	3,145	3,105	5,000
Anglo-Egyptian Sudan		2,500 3/	.7	—	—	—	—	—	—
Kenya	Dec. 31 1/	3,274 3/	3,148	3,075	3,160	3,232	3,300	—	—
Tanganyika	Mar. 31	1,780	2,001	2,019	2,216	2,366	2,316	—	—
Uganda		1,285	1,007	995	1,008	1,037	—	—	—
Basutoland		1,443 3/4/	1,545	1,545	1,703	—	—	—	—
Egypt	June	1,771 3/	1,350	1,385	—	—	1,400	1,200	—
French Morocco 10/	Dec. 31 1/	9,976	12,172	10,860	8,620	6,031	7,423	8,474	9,500
French West Africa and Togo		8,674	8,570	8,260	—	—	9,100	—	—
Madagascar 10/	Dec. 31 1/	193	202	174	161	156	158	177	204
Mozambique	Dec. 31 1/	84	67	62	56	58	65	64	—
Northern Rhodesia	Dec. 31 1/	36	29	35	34	35	38	36	—
Southern Rhodesia	Dec. 31 1/	310	305	334	330	325	286	302	—
South West Africa		2,972 3/4/	3,534	—	—	—	—	—	—
Spanish Morocco 10/		481	577	596	143	574	600	—	—
Tunisia 10/	Dec. 31 1/	3,026	3,250	3,324	2,976	1,788	1,752	1,587	1,894
Union of South	August	33,899 4/	17,888	—	—	—	—	—	—
Estimated total		100,000	101,400	96,400	91,500	86,100	90,000	89,600	91,800
OCEANIA									
Australia	Mar. 31	112,571 1/	120,209	105,371	96,396	95,723	102,559	108,728	115,000
New Zealand	Apr. 30	31,352 3/	32,976	33,975	33,000	32,682	32,483	32,845	33,000
Estimated total		144,000	153,200	139,400	129,400	128,400	135,100	141,600	148,000
Estimated world total		747,000	754,500	715,400	700,400	631,600	719,600	723,800	730,100

1/ End of year estimates (October to December) included under following year for comparisons and totals. Thus, for Canada the December 1, 1944 estimate of 2,822,000 head is shown under 1945. 2/ Preliminary. 3/ Average for 2 to 4 years only. 4/ Census or estimate for single year. 5/ June. 6/ March. 7/ Official statistics; may be underestimates of actual numbers. 8/ Totals for Western Germany and Soviet Zone. 9/ Census, December 31, 1940. 10/ Data include only number taxed. 11/ Includes China Proper (22 provinces), Manchuria, Jehol and Sinkiang (Turkestan). 12/ The census of May 10-12, 1947, reported 50,857,000 sheep on farms.

Office of Foreign Agricultural Relations. Prepared or estimated on the basis of official statistics of foreign governments, reports of United States foreign service officers, and other information. Data for countries having changed boundaries relate to present territory, unless otherwise noted. Totals include estimates for countries for which official statistics are unavailable.

and spring of 1946 and 1947 and the delayed return of pasture lands
from wartime cultivation. Sheep raising in Europe has not been
emphasized to the same extent as other livestock. Consequently,
recovery in the western European countries has been somewhat slower
than for hogs and cattle. Because of less dependence upon grain;
however, the upward trend in sheep numbers in Europe is expected to
continue even after hog production levels off. It is believed that
the eastern and southeastern European countries have been slow in
returning to prewar levels for the same reason.

Sheep numbers in the Soviet Union now are estimated to be above
their prewar level. This increase is attributed to some recovery of
numbers in the war-devastated areas and to acquisition from outside
areas.

Improved pastoral conditions in Australia and New Zealand have
enabled sheep producers, particularly in Australia, to expand their
flocks materially. Continuing high prices for wool have been the
principal inducement in Australia, while relatively high prices for
mutton and lamb in the U.K.-New Zealand agreement have furnished
sufficient incentive for maintaining flocks at a high level in
New Zealand.

In Asia, sheep numbers are relatively close to their 1936-40
level. Iranian numbers declined in 1949 and are considerably below
their 1936-40 average, while Iraqian numbers are above. Although
numbers in Turkey are considerably above the 1936-40 level, the
current estimate reflects a substantial decrease, but continues to
be above the long-time average. African numbers increased during
1949, particularly in Algeria and French Morocco.

This is one of a series of regularly scheduled reports on world
agricultural production approved by the Office of Foreign Agricultural
Relations Committee on Foreign Crop and Livestock Statistics. For this
report, the Committee was composed of C.M. Purves, Acting Chairman,
Elmer A. Reese, Eugene T. Ransom, Mary E. Long and Glenn A. Ruggles.

U. S. FOREIGN TRADE IN AGRICULTURAL PRODUCTS DURING FEBRUARY 1950 1/

United States exports of agricultural products during February, the eighth month of the 1949-50 fiscal year, were valued at $246,012,000 compared with $224,318,000 during January and with $338,323,000 during February last year. The nation's exports of all commodities, both agricultural and nonagricultural, were valued at $761,447,000 during February. Agricultural products accounted for 32 percent of the total.

Cotton continued to hold first place in value of agricultural exports during the month, the total amounting to $102,080,000 compared with $83,545,000 during the preceding month and $85,049,000 during February a year ago. Wheat and wheat flour were in second position, exports being valued at $48,866,000 compared with $47,313,000 in the preceding month and $104,148,000 in February a year ago. Third place this month was again held by corn, but the exports were valued at only $12,920,000 compared with $14,744,000 in January and $22,250,000 in February last year.

On a quantitative basis, the outstanding features of the February agricultural exports, compared with those for the same month a year ago, were the increases in a number of items (especially pork, lard, tallow, cotton, apples, pears, prunes, raisins and currants, grain sorghums, hops, soybean oil and white potatoes), and the substantial reductions in certain other items (especially dairy products, citrus fruits, canned fruits, barley and malt, rice, wheat and wheat flour, peanuts, soybeans, field and garden seeds, tobacco, dried beans and peas and canned vegetables).

United States imports of agricultural products during February 1950 were valued at $293,072,000 compared with $290,705,000 during January and with $238,221,000 during February last year. The nation's imports of all commodities, both agricultural and nonagricultural, were valued at $588,653,000 during the month under review. Agricultural products accounted for approximately 50 percent of the total. Heading the list this month were coffee, wool and sugar. Of special interest is the fact that the United States during February this year was a net importer of agricultural products to the extent of $47,060,000 while during February last year the country figured as a net exporter to the extent of $100,102,000.

On a quantitative basis, the outstanding developments in the February imports of agricultural products, compared with February 1949, were the substantial increases in a number of items (especially casein and lactarene, cheese, hides and skins, wool, barley malt, hops, copra, coconut oil, potatoes, cocoa or cacao beans, and spices). On the other hand, imports of pineapples, shelled almonds, coconut meat, castor beans, palm oil, tung oil, molasses, fresh tomatoes, coffee and rubber show substantial reductions compared with February last year.

1/ The publication U. S. Foreign Trade in Agricultural Products, containing fuller trade data than this summary presents, is published regularly and distributed free upon request by the Office of Foreign Agricultural Relations, U. S. Department of Agriculture, Washington 25, D. C.

UNITED STATES: Summary of exports, domestic, of selected agricultural products, during February 1949 and 1950

Commodity exported	Unit	February Quantity 1949	February Quantity 1950	Value 1949	Value 1950
		Thousands	Thousands	1,000 dollars	1,000 dollars
ANIMAL PRODUCTS:					
Butter	Lb.	311	251	224	162
Cheese	Lb.	4,728	269	1,919	119
Milk, condensed	Lb.	7,322	2,869	1,558	636
Milk, whole, dried	Lb.	8,229	3,654	4,149	1,754
Nonfat dry milk solids	Lb.	15,620	6,775	2,449	935
Milk, evaporated	Lb.	31,795	14,306	4,220	1,828
Eggs, dried	Lb.	1,267	46	984	38
Beef and veal, total 1/	Lb.	984	1,078	310	443
Pork, total 1/	Lb.	3,076	4,179	1,147	1,201
Horse meat	Lb.	2,870	1,706	441	260
Lard (including neutral)	Lb.	42,517	68,583	7,496	8,315
Tallow, edible and inedible	Lb.	18,365	27,385	2,320	2,072
VEGETABLE PRODUCTS:					
Cotton,unmfd,excl. linters (480 lb.)	Bale	518	679	85,049	102,080
Apples, fresh	Lb.	7,208	33,940	592	1,796
Grapefruit, fresh	Lb.	17,240	8,825	464	394
Oranges, fresh	Lb.	29,617	25,390	1,493	1,506
Pears, fresh	Lb.	1,775	2,127	141	200
Prunes, dried	Lb.	9,332	31,619	986	3,354
Raisins and currants	Lb.	8,166	26,188	764	2,227
Fruits, canned	Lb.	5,787	4,566	942	608
Fruit juices	Gal.	1,207	1,355	1,389	1,313
Barley, grain (48 lb.)	Bu.	2,268	331	3,159	394
Barley malt (34 lb.)	Bu.	385	219	1,028	559
Corn, grain (56 lb.)	Bu.	13,030	8,601	22,250	12,920
Grain sorghums (56 lb.)	Bu.	1,165	2,059	1,773	2,868
Rice, milled, brown, etc.	Lb.	66,740	36,432	6,110	2,420
Wheat, grain (60 lb.)	Bu.	30,771	19,240	79,042	42,430
Flour, wholly of U.S. wheat (100 lb.)	Bag	4,774	1,164	25,037	4,938
Flour, other (100 lb.)	Bag	10	279	69	1,498
Hops	Lb.	1,189	1,668	948	1,327
Peanuts, shelled	Lb.	67,588	10,680	11,074	903
Soybeans (except canned)	Lb.	66,148	59,624	3,096	2,429
Soybean oil, crude and refined	Lb.	13,041	37,359	2,587	4,601
Soya flour	Lb.	383	224	24	12
Seeds, field and garden	Lb.	8,989	1,561	2,939	614
Tobacco, bright flue-cured	Lb.	26,585	15,363	14,860	7,531
Tobacco, leaf, other	Lb.	9,060	3,685	4,613	1,880
Beans, dried	Lb.	28,980	3,717	2,652	304
Peas, dried	Lb.	10,682	2,488	1,168	133
Potatoes, white	Lb.	4,360	72,430	128	439
Vegetables, canned	Lb.	7,965	5,746	1,080	796
Total above				302,674	220,237
Food exported for relief, etc.				2,213	4,049
Other agricultural products				33,436	21,726
Total agricultural				338,323	246,012
Total all commodities				1,033,310	761,447

1/ Product weight. Compiled from official records, Bureau of the Census.

UNITED STATES: Summary of imports for consumption
of selected agricultural products during February 1949 and 1950

Commodity imported SUPPLEMENTARY	Unit	February Quantity 1949	1950	Value 1949	1950
ANIMALS AND ANIMAL PRODUCTS:		Thousands	Thousands	1,000 dollars	1,000 dollars
Cattle, dutiable	No.	12	33	1,838	4,950
Cattle, free (for breeding)	No.	1	1	396	397
Casein and lactarene	Lb.	2,003	5,398	417	708
Cheese	Lb.	1,533	6,845	895	2,359
Hides and skins	Lb.	9,639	19,933	4,674	6,845
Beef canned, incl. corned	Lb.	6,612	6,920	2,278	2,139
Wool, unmfd,excl. free, etc. ,......	Lb.	23,994	38,054	16,166	22,084
VEGETABLE PRODUCTS:					
Cotton,unmfd.,excl.linters (480 lb.)	Bale	8	71	723	14,470
Jute and jute butts,unmfd.(2,240 lb.)	Ton	8	3	3,193	768
Apples, green or ripe (50 lb.)	Bu.	189	344	531	698
Olives in brine	Gal.	754	856	1,585	1,425
Pineapples, prep. or preserved	Lb.	4,391	2,767	498	315
Barley malt	Lb.	7,493	8,675	375	412
Hops	Lb.	244	1,478	251	1,787
Almonds, shelled	Lb.	1,161	125	373	41
Brazil or cream nuts, not shelled ...	Lb.	0	0	0	0
Cashew nuts	Lb.	1,440	1,741	626	570
Coconut meat, shredded, etc.	Lb.	8,542	6,434	1,572	1,091
Castor beans	Lb.	35,846	26,605	2,047	1,361
Copra	Lb.	41,276	54,321	4,547	4,509
Flaxseed (56 lb.)	Bu.	20	2	110	6
Coconut oil	Lb.	6,950	10,729	1,250	1,422
Palm oil	Lb.	7,263	2,263	1,115	217
Tung oil	Lb.	11,323	3,758	2,202	840
Sugar, excl. beet (2,000 lb.)	Ton	339	272	32,660	27,614
Molasses, unfit for human consumption	Gal.	18,440	14,049	1,419	946
Tobacco, cigarette leaf	Lb.	5,022	4,584	3,278	3,293
Tobacco, other leaf	Lb.	1,271	1,137	1,874	1,789
Potatoes, white	Lb.	40,395	50,430	988	1,103
Tomatoes, natural state	Lb.	49,449	37,471	3,897	2,213
COMPLEMENTARY					
Wool, unmfd., free in bond	Lb.	15,752	36,598	5,654	12,997
VEGETABLE PRODUCTS:					
Bananas	Bunch	3,261	3,486	2,943	3,546
Coffee (ex. into Puerto Rico)	Lb.	219,783	207,832	57,316	84,241
Cocoa or cacao beans and shells	Lb.	51,483	94,469	14,475	19,713
Tea	Lb.	7,606	7,943	3,699	3,801
Spices (complementary)	Lb.	4,994	6,220	1,591	3,978
Sisal and henequen (2,240 lb.)	Ton	8	10	2,615	2,626
Rubber, crude	Lb.	128,074	119,600	22,580	18,991
Total above				202,651	256,265
Other agricultural products				35,570	36,807
Total agricultural products				238,221	293,072
Total all commodities				554,673	588,653

Compiled from official records, Bureau of the Census.

COMMODITY DEVELOPMENTS

TOBACCO

BELGIUM'S TOBACCO CONSUMPTION AND IMPORTS STEADY

Belgium's 1949 consumption and imports of leaf tobacco were near the levels of the previous 2 years, according to the American Embassy in Brussels.

Leaf used in the domestic manufacture of tobacco products in 1949 totaled 52.8 million pounds, compared with 51.2 million in 1948 and 48.9 million in 1947. The quantity of leaf used in the manufacture of various tobacco products in 1949 was as follows: cigarettes, 25.8 million pounds; smoking tobacco, 23.1 million pounds; cigarillos, 2.0 million pounds; cigars, 1.4 million pounds; and chewing tobacco and snuff, 0.5 million pounds. There has been no substantial change in the proportion of leaf used in the various manufactured products during the past 3 years.

BELGIUM: Imports of leaf tobacco, by sources, 1949 with comparisons

Country of Origin	1947	1948	1949
	1,000 pounds	1,000 pounds	1,000 pounds
United States............:	25,344	28,356	25,296
Dominican Republic.........:	3,001	2,328	3,485
Brazil....................:	3,032	2,751	3,106
Turkey....................:	880	1,307	3,014
Paraguay..................:	942	1,045	1,572
India.....................:	1,951	1,307	1,475
Argentina.................:	2,303	1,232	774
Bulgaria..................:	63	346	509
Indonesia.................:	29	229	443
Philippine Republic.......:	123	357	351
Colombia..................:	236	262	207
Southern Rhodesia.........:	65	260	196
Other Countries...........:	1,725	1/ 2,004	1,420
Total............:	39,694	41,784	41,848

1/ Includes 628,000 pounds of stemmed leaf, much of which came from countries designated above.

Official and U. S. Foreign Service reports.

Belgium's imports of leaf in 1949 totaled 41.8 million pounds. This compares with 41.8 million in 1948 and 39.7 million in 1947. The United States was the principal source of leaf, supplying 25.3 million pounds, or 60 percent of the 1949 total. Imports from the United States in 1948 totaled 28.4 million and in 1947 about 25.3 million pounds. The Dominican Republic was the second most important source of leaf in 1949, supplying 3.5 million pounds, or 8 percent of the total. Other important sources of leaf in 1949 include Brazil, Turkey, Paraguay, India, Argentina and Bulgaria. In addition to leaf, Belgium in 1949 imported 593,000 pounds of cigarettes, 470,000 pounds of smoking tobacco and 117,000 pounds of cigars and cigarillos.

TROPICAL PRODUCTS

INDONESIAN TEA PRODUCTION AND EXPORTS HIGHER

In 1949, Indonesia produced 59.8 million pounds of tea, and exported 47.2 million, according to the American Embassy in Djakarta. This is more than double Indonesia's 1948 production of 27.8 million and exports of 18.6 million pounds of tea, but only about a third as large as the prewar (1935-39) average production of 170.1 million and exports of 153.2 million pounds.

There were few significant changes from the 1948 pattern of trade. The Netherlands continued to provide the largest market, taking 28.7 million pounds in 1949 compared with 11.3 million in 1948. Egypt and the Anglo-Egyptian Sudan replaced the United States as the second largest market in 1949, with shipments of 7.2 million pounds compared with only 5.2 million for the United States. In 1948, Indonesia exported 3.9 million pounds of tea to the United States and 1.2 million to Egypt and the Anglo-Egyptian Sudan. Other important destinations for Indonesia's 1949 tea shipments were Ireland, the United Kingdom, Canada Iraq, and Iran.

The outlook for continued recovery of tea production in Indonesia is promising. The 1950 harvest has been forecast at 77 million pounds. An Indonesian official has estimated that it is possible to increase tea production in Indonesia to 160 million pounds by 1954. While it is doubtful that the total area planted in tea will be greatly extended during the next few years, the yield per acre is expected to increase steadily as a larger proportion of the total estate area is brought back into production. The degree of recovery depends in large measure on the maintenance of political and economic stability, solution of labor problems, and acquisition of a larger supply of fertilizer for tea estates and adequate equipment for tea factories.

INDONESIA: Exports of tea, 1949 with comparisons

Destination	Average 1935-39	1947	1948 1/	1949 1/
	1,000 pounds	1,000 pounds	1,000 pounds	1,000 pounds
United States	20,399	29	3,896	5,174
Canada	162	-	57	778
Other America	5,944	-	175	179
Netherlands	31,378	955	11,261	28,651
Ireland	2/	2/	2/	1,283
United Kingdom	26,052	2	22	937
Other Europe	5,125	363	525	157
Egypt and Anglo-Egyptian Sudan	11,906	1,101	1,202	7,183
Other Africa	8,986	-	89	877
Asia & Oceania	43,223	3,748	1,351	2,006
Total	153,175	6,198	18,578	42,225

1/ Preliminary
2/ Included in Other Europe

Reports of U.S. Foreign Service Officers and International
Tea Committee.

CEYLON'S TEA PRODUCTION AND EXPORTS CONTINUE AT HIGH LEVEL

Ceylon produced 298.5 million pounds of tea in 1949 and exported
297.6 million pounds, the American Embassy in Colombo reports. This
compares with production of 298.7 million pounds in 1948, 298.5 million
in 1947, and a prewar (1935-39) average of 231.5 million pounds and with
exports of 296.1 million pounds in 1948, 287.3 million in 1947, and a
prewar average of 221.6 million pounds.

The United Kingdom remained Ceylon's best tea customer, taking
120.5 million pounds in 1949 compared with 97.9 million pounds in 1948.
Australia replaced the United States as the second leading market in
1949. Ceylon exported 33.8 million pounds of tea to Australia in 1949
and 36.0 million in 1948 compared with shipments to the United States of
26.4 million pounds in 1949 and 41.9 million in 1948. Other important
destinations for Ceylon's 1949 tea exports were Egypt, Union of South
Africa, Canada, and New Zealand.

The big question presently confronting the Ceylon tea industry is
whether or not there will be a bulk purchase contract for 1950 with the
United Kingdom Ministry of Food. The United Kingdom consumes nearly half
of Ceylon's annual tea output, and the Ceylon trade feels that past
contracts have given firmness and stability to the Colombo tea market.

CEYLON: Exports of tea, 1949 with comparisons

Destination	Average 1935-39	1947	1948 1/	1949 1/
	Million pounds	Million pounds	Million pounds	Million pounds
United Kingdom	150.9	107.6	97.9	120.5
Australia	12.6	32.4	36.0	33.8
United States	13.0	20.9	41.9	26.4
Egypt	3.2	26.2	26.2	25.0
Union of South Africa	10.4	18.3	18.2	15.6
Canada	8.4	24.5	16.1	14.7
New Zealand	9.5	11.0	10.7	14.5
Other	13.6	46.4	49.1	47.3
Total	221.6	287.3	296.1	297.6

1/ Preliminary

Reports of U.S. Foreign Service Officers and International Tea Committee.

Another matter of great interest is the discussion of the possible opening of the London Tea Auctions in 1951. One of Ceylon's objections to the reopening of the Mincing Lane Auctions is the loss of dollar earnings because of resales by London to the United States.

COTTON AND OTHER FIBER

REGISTRATION FOR THE BRITISH RE-EQUIPMENT FINANCIAL AID TO SPINNING MILLS CLOSED APRIL 5, 1950

As April 5, 1950, is the final date for participation in the British Government's program for granting financial aid for modernization of cotton spinning mills, the Manchester Financial Times has made a survey of the response of the mills to the Government's offer. It is assumed the Government will make some type of final report on results of the Re-equipment Subsidy Act of 1948 at a later date, but the Financial Time's survey of April 2, 1950, presents information of interest meanwhile.

The number of groups approved for registration under the Re-equipment Subsidy Act was 28 as of April 2, 1950, representing 283 mills, which account altogether for slightly over 21 million spindles or 55 percent of those in place in the industry on August 16, 1945.

The Board of Trade has approved modernization plans for 60 mills
and proposals for another 75 mills are under consideration. Plans
could be submitted and approved for subsidy after the qualifying
date for registration and any group could, presumably, ask for approval when its re-equipment had been carried out. However, only
machinery ordered by April 5, 1950, and delivered between August 16,
1945, and April 1952 will qualify for the 25 percent subsidy.

(See Cotton-Price Quotations on Page 403)

GRAINS, GRAIN PRODUCTS AND FEEDS

PERU RELINQUISHES GOVERNMENT
MONOPOLY OF WHEAT PURCHASES

Peruvian flour mills were given permission to purchase wheat on
their own account in a decree dated March 13, 1950, according to the
Agricultural Attache, American Embassy, Lima. Previously, the
Ministry of Agriculture made all purchases of both imported and
locally grown wheat, and the mills were operated on a contract basis
to the Government. The decree transfers the purchase of wheat from
the Peruvian Government to local millers.

The decree authorizes the 4 Peruvian flour mills to purchase
directly both from foreign countries and from local producers. The
mills are limited in their purchase abroad to the terms of the
International Wheat Agreement and the Commercial and Financial Agreement with Argentina. The prices paid for wheat from Argentina, however, may not exceed those paid for wheat imported under the International Wheat Agreement.

Locally-grown wheat is to be given preference and the producer
is guaranteed the international price for home-grown wheat of the
same quality and weight per bushel. Mills are obliged to maintain
at least a 2-months stock of wheat for milling. The Government of
Peru will guarantee the mills a subsidy to cover the difference
between the actual cost of the flour made and the sales price which
is fixed by the Government.

The mills are required to obtain approval of foreign purchases
of wheat, but this is not expected to cause any serious handicap to
the millers. The decree meets with the general approval of Peruvian
wheat millers. The preference to be given to locally-grown wheat
will be an inspiration to Peruvian producers even though it is not
likely that their product will equal the quality and bushel weight of
wheat imported from the United States and Canada, it was stated.

CANADA ANNOUNCES 1950-51
GRAIN PRICES

Canada's Minister of Trade and Commerce, on April 5 announced the initial advance to be made to producers for western wheat, oats, and barley for the crop year beginning August 1, 1950. The initial price for wheat was set at $1.40 per bushel in Canadian currency (about $1.27 in U.S. currency). The price is, as usual, based on No. 1 Northern in store Ft. William Port Arthur. The final price producers receive, of course, will depend on the world price for wheat during the season, since profits accruing from the Wheat Board's sales are returned to growers.

The new advance was set at a lower rate than the initial payment for recent years, which was $1.75 per bushel in Canadian currency. Press reports indicate that producers were disappointed that the rate was lowered at this time when farmers' costs are comparatively high.

Initial prices for western feed grains are to be unchanged from the present advance rate of 65 cents per bushel (Canadian) for No. 2 oats and 93 cents for No. 3 six-row barley. Prices for these grains, also, are based on grain in store at Ft. William/Port Arthur.

BELGIUM, THE NETHERLANDS AND WESTERN
GERMANY INCREASE RICE IMPORTS

During 1949, Belgium imported 30,372 short tons of rice, about half the prewar level, but 3 times the 1948 imports. The United States supplied half the 1949 volume, with Egypt the next most important source. In 1948, out of 9,500 short tons imported, 8,025 tons came from Brazil.

The following table shows 1949 rice imports into Belgium by country of origin.

Country	Short tons
United States	14,729
Egypt	9,173
Thailand	2,416
Brazil	1,302
Belgian Congo	1,247
Argentina	539
Surinam	442
Curacao	288
Italy	216
Other countries	20
Total	30,372

Rice imports into the Netherlands during 1949 totaled 32,000 short tons (milled basis) or just slightly above the Belgian figure. Year-end stocks were about 1,100 tons and after taking small opening stocks and some reexports into account, apparent consumption was 30,500 tons. This would provide a per capita consumption of just over 6 pounds annually compared to the prewar (1936-38) average of 13 pounds.

Thailand supplied the bulk of the 1949 imports while Burma was the largest supplier in 1948. Indonesia shipped 5,669 short tons, or about 19 percent of total imports in 1949 against only 10 tons in 1948.

In prewar years, the Netherlands imported mainly rough and brown rice. In 1949, however, two-thirds of the imports were fully milled. Imports during 1949 by country of origin are shown below:

Country	Short tons
Indonesia	5,669
Thailand	16,846
Italy	7,418
Surinam	2,108
Curacao	103
United States	7
Other countries	9
Total	32,160

Rice imports into Western Germany during 1949 totaled 52,541 short tons (exclusive of the French Zone Jan.-Sept. 1949). A few tons of ground rice and rice starch were also imported. Stocks on hand as of December 31 were reported at 20,000 tons. As there were no stocks at the beginning of the year, apparent consumption was just over 32,000 tons or about 1½ pounds per capita. While this is considerably below the prewar rate, rice has not been an important food item in Western Germany.

Imports during 1949, including polished and unpolished (semi-milled) rice are shown below by country of origin:

Country	Short tons
Belgian Congo	500
Brazil	33
Egypt	6,530
Indonesia	843
Italy	42,052
Netherlands	621
Surinam	1,629
Thailand	29
United States	289
Other countries	15
Total	52,541

About 80 percent of Western Germany's rice came from Italy and the
bulk of the Italian imports (mostly semi-milled) arrived in the last
quarter of 1949. This accounts for the fairly substantial stocks at
the end of the year and the very low per capita consumption during the
year.

BURMA'S RICE
EXPORTS DECLINE

Rice exports from Burma during the first quarter of 1950 totaled
337 million pounds, or approximately one-third the 961 million pounds
exported during the corresponding period of 1949. Shipments in January,
February, and March dropped to 33, 84, and 220 million pounds, compared
with exports during the corresponding months of 1949 of 217, 412, and
332 million pounds, respectively.

The decrease in exports is attributed to a depletion of stocks at
ports at the beginning of the year, and a delay in negotiating a satis-
factory price agreement with importing countries for the 1949-50 crop.
Exports will probably show a rise as stocks are transported from surplus
areas to the ports and as arrangements are completed with respect to
prices. So far during the season, Japan has contracted for a relatively
large volume of rice from Burma.

LIBERIA TO INCREASE
RICE ACREAGE

The acreage planted to rice in Liberia in 1950 is expected to be
somewhat larger than the 800,000 acres sown in 1949, according to a
preliminary survey of the United States Economic Mission. The planting
season will begin in April, about one month earlier than usual, because
of early rains. Most of the planting will be on upland soil, although
areas planted on swamp land are being increased in accordance with the
better land-use practice recommended by the Liberian Department of
Agriculture. United States exports of rice to Liberia approximate 5
million pounds annually.

FATS AND OILS

OUTLOOK FOR AFRICAN GROUNDNUT
SCHEME CROPS DISAPPOINTING

The third season's plantings of peanuts and sunflowers under the
British East African Groundnut Scheme in Tanganyika again are being
threatened by a serious drought. According to the American Consulate,
Dar es Salaam, by the beginning of the last week in March, the effects
of the maldistribution and shortage of rainfall--although the total for
the season as of the close of February was somewhat better than at the
corresponding time last year--were particularly evident in the Kongwa
region of the Central Province where the dominant share of the Scheme's

total acreage in oilseed crops is planted. Under the direction of the
British Overseas Food Corporation an over-all total of about 82,000 acres
had been planted by March 21. Of this area about three-fourths had been
planted to sunflowers--much of this on newly cleared land, the remainder
on land planted to peanuts in the 2 previous seasons.

In the Kongwa region, where total plantings approximated 69,000
acres by the last week in March, a late start in the rainy season had
prompted the decision at the Scheme's headquarters to plant 9,000 acres
of sunflowers in December before the rains. This experiment did not
prove entirely successful, however, and half of the acreage had to be
replanted. The rains began on December 23, 1949, and although planting
conditions were reportedly good in early January there were two subsequent
periods of drought which made it inadvisable to plant the total acreage
available at Kongwa. The first of these periods was from January 18 to
February 4, and the second, beginning February 24, lasted at least 1
month. Consequently, whereas plans originally called for planting 80,000
acres in the Kongwa region alone, it appeared there would be a shortfall
there of some 10,000 acres.

Weeds also have been a problem at Kongwa. In January, when conditions
for their growth were highly favorable, all available tractors had to be
used for seed-bed preparation over the maximum possible acreage. Although
the weeds got an upper hand in a number of fields for a time, the situation
had been brought under control by late March.

Prospects for the crops in the Urambo region of Western Province as
of the latter part of March were more favorable than they were at Kongwa.
About 8,200 acres had been planted to sunflowers and roughly 2,800 acres
to peanuts. Recent rains had counteracted in part the effects of the
severe drought of the previous two weeks. Rosette disease, which had
contributed materially to the very low yields of 1949, appeared to be
virtually absent this year.

In the Nachingwea region of Southern Province, several trial plots
planted to peanuts, sunflowers, and maize did not look promising because
of the late start of rains. The total acreage of these plots is only
425 acres and they are in 9 separate areas of the 420,000 acres which
are planned for development and cultivation in the next 5 years.

Although the 1950 outlook for the East African Groundnut Scheme's
crops was disappointing as of late March because of the dry spells, there
is still possibility that the crop may turn out better than conditions
at that time indicated.

PHILIPPINE COPRA EXPORTS
INCREASE IN MARCH

Exports of copra from the Philippine Republic during March 1950, totaling 43,185 long tons, represent a 45-percent increase over the February shipments of 29,736 tons. During January-March, exports totaled 110,931 tons compared with 104,271 tons shipped in the comparable period of 1949. Approximately 75 percent of the March exports were to the United States.

PHILIPPINE REPUBLIC: Copra exports, March 1950 with comparisons
(Long tons)

Country of destination	Average 1935-39	1949 1/	Jan-Mar 1950 1/	March 1949 1/	March 1950 1/
United States (total)..	206,801	375,071	81,959	20,690	31,585
Atlantic Coast....	-	39,023	10,102	-	6,481
Gulf Coast........	-	43,098	17,452	4,929	5,783
Pacific Coast.....	-	292,950	54,405	15,761	19,321
Canada...............	-	13,900	5,750	450	3,300
Mexico...............	7,260	-	-	-	-
Panama Canal Zone....	-	775	-	-	-
Panama, Republic of...	-	209	-	-	-
Colombia.............	-	4,000	1,850	-	-
Venezuela............	-	1,133	1,500	-	-
Belgium..............	10	7,650	6,779	-	1,000
Denmark..............	6,025	16,085	-	2,000	-
France...............	24,589	23,757	-	8,900	-
Western Germany.......	7,309	28,510	393	4,086	-
Italy................	4,079	17,839	3,300	2,712	2,300
Netherlands..........	28,415	10,850	4,000	-	4,000
Norway...............	91	8,000	3,000	-	-
Poland...............	-	1,500	-	1,500	-
Sweden...............	4,183	7,600	-	1,000	-
Switzerland..........	-	1,100	-	-	-
Japan................	1,047	6,075	500	-	500
Israel and Palestine..	-	4,974	1,000	-	-
Syria................	-	1,800	500	-	500
Egypt................	1,271	-	-	-	-
Union of South Africa.	-	2,198	300	712	-
Others...............	8,758	23,596	100	100	-
Total...........	299,838	556,613	2/110,931	42,150	43,185

1/ Preliminary. 2/ January and February figures revised (see text).

American Embassy, Manila.

Further revisions have been received on the January and February copra exports. The 500 tons reported shipped to the Republic of Panama in January actually were sent to Venezuela. February shipments were revised upward to 29,736 tons and the total to Norway changed to 1,500 tons.

March coconut oil shipments of 3,789 tons were destined to the United States. A correction of the January exports of coconut oil disclose that the 200 tons reported as consigned to the Republic of Panama were sent to Venezuela.

PHILIPPINE REPUBLIC: Coconut oil exports, March 1950 with comparisons
(Long tons)

Country of destination	Average: 1935-39	1949 1/	Jan.-Mar.: 1950 1/	March 1949 1/	March 1950 1/
United States.........	155,358	51,864	9,519	3,269	3,789
Canada...............	1,885	-	-	-	-
Norway...............	-	500	-	-	-
Western Germany......	660	3,830	-	963	-
Italy................	-	4,249	-	285	-
Netherlands..........	-	1,409	-	195	-
China................	392	73	-	-	-
Hong Kong............	583	-	-	-	-
Poland...............	-	260	-	-	-
Thailand.............	54	-	-	-	-
Union of South Africa.	-	1,390	329	-	-
Other countries......	2,815	572	238	-	-
Total............	161,747	64,147	10,086	4,712	3,789

1/ Preliminary.

American Embassy, Manila

Total shipments of copra and coconut oil in terms of copra during March amounted to 49,200 tons.

The copra export price on April 14 was quoted at $200 per short ton c.i.f. Pacific Coast compared with $192.50 in March. Local buying prices at Manila were reported at 39 to 40 pesos per 100 kilograms ($198.13 to $203.20 per long ton) and in producing regions at 37 to 39 pesos ($187.97 to $198.13).

MALAYAN COPRA, COCONUT OIL
EXPORTS INCREASE IN 1949

Exports of copra from the Federation of Malaya during 1949, totaling 39,325 long tons, represent an increase of 51 percent over 1948. Approximately 96 percent of the 1949 exports went to Europe with Poland taking 20 percent, compared with Europe's share in the previous year of 91 percent and Sweden taking the largest quantity.

Coconut oil shipments of 61,226 tons were 13 percent greater than during 1948. India, which took only 299 tons during 1948, accounted for 24,606 tons in 1949 or 40 percent of the total exports.

Exports of copra and coconut oil in terms of copra during 1949 amounted to 186,509 tons, representing an increase of 37 percent over the 1948 total of 135,669 tons.

MALAYA: Copra exports and imports, 1949 with comparisons

(Long tons)

Country	Average 1935-39	1948	1949 1/
Exports			
Austria.......................	-	-	6,486
Czechoslovakia..........	652	600	2,575
Denmark....................	2,050	7,453	15,495
France......................	8,573	2,196	3,490
Italy........................	11,322	8,247	3,900
Netherlands..............	28,956	11,323	16,454
Norway.....................	4,703	750	9,532
Poland......................	3,358	6,020	16,577
Sweden.....................	1,850	13,738	2,051
United Kingdom.........	57,750	2,081	5,095
Other Europe............	49,209	1,480	4,231
Morocco....................	493	1,873	300
Asia........................	3,977	2,664	3,139
Other countries.........	18,793	616	-
Total.............	191,691	59,041	89,325
Imports			
British possessions...	10,617	5,454	21,079
Indonesia...............	105,500	81,330	90,958
Other countries........	2,134	882	1,712
Total.............	118,251	37,666	113,749

1/ Preliminary.

American Consulate General, Singapore.

Imports of copra into Malaya in 1949 amounted to 113,749 tons, a 13-percent increase over the volume for the previous year, and 27 percent greater than the total exports. Over 80 percent of the total imports came from Indonesia. Only 722 tons of coconut oil were imported during the year under review against 3,031 tons in 1948. Most of the oil also originated in Indonesia.

Imports of copra and coconut oil, in copra equivalent, in 1949 totaled 114,895 tons showing an increase of 24 percent over the 92,477 tons imported during the previous year.

Malayan net exports of copra and coconut oil, on a copra basis, were therefore 71,614 tons against 43,192 tons during 1948 and 147,306 tons as the prewar average.

MALAYA: Coconut oil exports and imports, 1949 with comparisons

(Long tons)

Country	Average 1935-39	1948	1949 1/
Exports			
France............:	100	2,194	1,456
Italy.............:	20	8,198	4,064
Netherlands.......:	822	3,488	5,574
Sweden............:	185	2,200	-
United Kingdom....:	8,857	3,334	-
Other Europe.....:	290	3,895	2,783
U.S.S.R...........:	-	2,700	3,100
Burma.............:	3,908	3,828	3,877
Hong Kong.........:	1,391	8,031	4,471
India.............:	22,500	299	24,606
Indonesia.........:	3,119	374	966
Iraq..............:	-	937	1,427
Pakistan..........:		2,111	2,187
Other Asia........:	1,772	474	2,020
Egypt.............:	3,295	3,821	4,070
Other countries...:	850	2,392	625
Total.........:	47,109	48,276	61,226
Imports			
British possessions..:	16	174	55
Indonesia.........:	328	2,857	667
Other countries...:	229	-	-
Total.........:	573	3,031	722

1/ Preliminary.

American Consulate General, Singapore.

WHALE CATCH EXCEEDS PREVIOUS SEASON'S TOTAL;
WHALING COMMISION TO MEET IN OSLO

The total catch of baleen whales in the Antarctic during the
1949-50 pelagic whaling season--which lasted from December 22 through
March 15--was 16,011 blue whale units. This total, reported to the
U. S. Department of Interior's Fish and Wildlife Service by the
International Bureau of Whaling Statistics, Sandefjord, Norway, exceeds slightly the reported catch of 15,926 blue whale units for the
1948-49 season.

The blue whale is the basis for measuring the total catch because blue-whales yield the largest quantity of oil. According to
provisions of the International Agreement for the Regulation of
Whaling, drawn up at the time of the International Whaling Convention
held in Washington, D. C., December 2, 1946, the following shall
be considered the equivalent of a blue whale: two fin-back whales,
2.5 hump-back whales, or 6 sei whales.

The International Whaling Commission--consisting of a
representative of each of the 14 countries signatory to the International Agreement--is scheduled to convene its 1950 meeting in
Oslo, Norway, tentatively on July 18. The United States, a party
to the Agreement, will be represented by Commissioner A. Remington
Kellogg.

UNITED STATES OLIVE OIL
IMPORTS DROP IN 1949

United States imports of edible olive oil in 1949 amounted to
10,025 short tons, 44 percent less than in 1948 and 68 percent less
than prewar. Over 47 percent of the 1949 total came from Italy,
29 percent from Spain, and 10 percent from French Morocco. Only
1,562 tons of inedible olive oil were imported the past year
compared with 4,887 in 1948 and 17,724 prewar. Italy accounted
for over 90 percent of the 1949 total.

Effective February 25, 1950, all types of olive oil were re-
moved from import control in the United States.

(See accompanying tables on following page)

UNITED STATES: EDIBLE OLIVE OIL IMPORTS, 1949 WITH COMPARISONS

(Short tons)

Country of origin	Average 1935-39	1946	1947	1948 1/	1949 1/
Algeria..............	126	-	-	217	170
France..............	2,432	-	7	27	115
French Morocco......	3	-	1,021	4,786	1,042
Greece..............	2,452	16	271	892	36
Italy...............	15,766	1,842	1,884	8,319	4,753
Portugal............	183	-	5	110	108
Spain...............	8,787	3,803	2,020	3,579	2,921
Syria and Lebanon...	18	590	355	46	134
Tunisia.............	1,600	-	-	-	445
Turkey..............	-	-	-	28	272
Other countries.....	38	79	62	47	28
Total.....	31,405	6,330	5,625	18,051	10,025

UNITED STATES: INEDIBLE OLIVE OIL IMPORTS, 1949 WITH COMPARISONS

(Short tons)

Country of origin	Average 1935-39	1946	1947	1948 1/	1949 1/
Algeria.............	3,996	-	-	-	-
France.............	51	-	-	-	-
French Morocco......	37	2	3	62	22
Greece.............	5,505	-	-	2,322	14
Italy..............	1,868	-	51	2,436	1,422
Portugal...........	1,930	-	-	-	-
Spain.............	2,144	14	-	27	4
Syria and Lebanon...	134	34	54	16	81
Tunisia............	1,975	2	-	-	19
Turkey.............	37	-	-	22	-
Other countries.....	47	-	16	2	-
Total.....	17,724	52	124	4,887	1,562

1/ Preliminary.

Compiled from official sources.

LIVESTOCK AND ANIMAL PRODUCTS

CANADIAN EGG OUTLOOK
IMPROVED

Greatly increased domestic consumption of eggs in Canada has improved the egg marketing problem and reduced the possibility of large egg exports to the United States. When the British egg contract, which had for years taken care of Canada's surplus, was not renewed in January, egg prices dropped sharply. A further decline, which might have reached a very undesirable low level, was checked by a government announcement of a support price program. The announced price was low, 38 cents per dozen for eggs in storage at the end of the season, but it served two useful purposes: It offered reasonable protection to producers, and allowed the price to decline sufficiently to stimulate consumption enough to eliminate the threat of an unwieldy surplus.

NEWCASTLE DISEASE
APPEARS IN BELGIUM

Newcastle disease in Belgium appeared during January on a poultry farm in East Flanders and is spreading seriously through much of the country. It is believed in the majority of cases that the germs of the disease are carried to poultry farms principally by crows, magpies, woodpigeons and also, by infected products and baskets brought to these farms. There is almost total mortality.

Poultry farmers have been told to refrain from purchasing poultry and eggs for hatching of unknown origin, as well as feed in sacks which may have been contaminated. As soon as the first symptoms of the disease appear, the farmer or owner of poultry is compelled to slaughter one of the infected birds and to send it at once in a water-proof wrapping to a laboratory for diagnosis. Rather complete controls have been set up to prevent the spread of the disease once it has been recognized. Provisions also have been made for vaccinations with living virus provided by the Government.

IMPORTS AND DISTRIBUTION OF
POWDERED MILK OPPOSED IN SPAIN

The Milk Producers' Conference in Spain has requested the Spanish Government through a recently adopted resolution to stop imports of powdered milk and ban its distribution to the public. The Conference felt that if sufficient attention were given to local dairying enough extra milk could be produced to compensate for the imported quantity of dry milk. Trade statistics are not available for 1949, but about 3.5 million pounds of powdered milk was imported in 1948 of which about 72 percent originated in Argentina.

MILK SURPLUS EXPECTED
IN ENGLAND

A milk surplus of 10 million gallons a month is expected above that needed for fluid milk consumption by the United Kingdom Ministry of Food during the May and June flush season.

Producers are establishing new monthly records. Consumption (which is at present around 2½ pints per week for non-priority users) has decreased in recent months. Thus more milk is expected than can be handled by present facilities.

Suggested alternatives to utilize the plentiful supply are a "drink more milk" campaign, a reduction in retail prices, or allow farmers to separate a portion of the milk they produce. The first suggestion has been described as of doubtful efficacy and the second would require an increase in subsidies contrary to current policy. The consideration of a scheme to decrease production will not be considered by government officials.

The total production of milk in England and Wales during March is expected to be around 138 million gallons. Fluid consumption is expected to have been about 117 million gallons.

URUGUAY SHIPS ONLY 74
BALES OF WOOL IN MARCH

The wool market in Uruguay remains practically paralyzed because of the continuing wool strike. The only shipments in March were to the United States and consisted of only 74 bales.

Sales during March were slow and price unchanged. The United States purchased 1,488 bales, predominantly new clip.

Exports for the 1949-50 season to the first of April were 37,270 bales to the United States, and 56,714 total. Exports for the same period last season were 29,183 bales and 67,088 bales, respectively.

AUSTRALIAN WOOL
SALES CALENDAR

The dates, selling center and quantities for sale for the remaining wool-selling season in Australia are given in the following table. It has also been announced that the 1950-51 season sales will start at Sydney on August 28, and at Adelaide on August 29.

May			:	June		
Date	Center	Bales	:	Date	Center	Bales
2/4	Geelong	28,000	:	1	Adelaide	(See May)
8/11	Sydney	36,000	:	1	Newcastle	(" ")
8/11	Melbourne	30,000	:	1	Goulburn	" "
9/10	Goulburn	6,000	:	1	Albury	" "
15	Perth	15,000	:	5/8	Sydney	36,000
15/18	Brisbane	60,000	:	5/8	Melbourne	X
15/19	Tasmania	13,000	:	12/15	Brisbane	60,000
22/26	Sydney	40,000	:	19/20	Adelaide	X
23/25	Geelong	28,000	:	19/22	Brisbane	60,000
29	Sydney	10,000	:	26	Ballarat	X
30/Jn. 1	Adelaide	40,000	:	26/27	Melbourne	X
do.	Newcastle	20,000/	:	26/29	Sydney	36,000
31/Jn. 1	Goulburn	5,000ϕ	:	28/29	Geelong	X
do.	Albury	8,000	:	29/30	Perth	X

/ - Approximately.

ϕ - Minimum

X - In Southern Centers, June Sale dates are tentative only and quantities undetermined.

COTTON AND OTHER FIBER
(Continued from Page 389)

COTTON-PRICE QUOTATIONS
ON WORLD MARKETS

  The following table shows certain cotton-price quotations on foreign markets converted at current rates of exchange.

COTTON: Spot prices in certain foreign markets, and the
U.S. gulf-port average

Market location kind, and quality	Date 1950	Unit of weight	Unit of currency	Price in foreign currency	Equivalent U.S. cent per pound
Alexandria		Kantar			
Ashmouni, Good...........	4-20	99.05 lbs.	Tallari	100.25	58.11
Ashmouni, F.G.F..........	"	"	"	97.25	56.37
Karnak, Good.............	"	"	"	76.65	44.43
Karnak, F.G.F............	"	"	"	70.15	40.66
Bombay		Candy			
Jarila, Fine.............	"	784 lbs.	Rupee	1/ 620.00	16.50
Broach Vijay, Fine.......	"	"	"	1/ 690.00	18.37
Karachi		Maund			
4F Punjab, S.G., Fine....	4-19	82.28 lbs.	"	74.50	27.32
239F Sind, S.G., Fine....	"	"	"	76.00	27.87
289F Punjab, S.G., Fine..	"	"	"	77.00	28.23
Buenos Aires		Metric ton			
Type B...................	4-20	2204.6 lbs.	Peso	1/ 4100.00	38.49
Lima		Sp. quintal			
Tanguis, Type 5..........	4-19	101.4 lbs.	Sol	(not quoted)	
Pima, Type 1.............	"	"	"	(not quoted)	
Recife		Arroba			
Mata, Type 4.............	4-20	33.07 lbs.	Cruzeiro	185.00	30.44
Sertao, Type 5...........	"	"	"	(not available	
Sertao, Type 4...........	"	"	"	225.00	37.02
Sao Paulo					
Sao Paulo, Type 5........	"	"	"	178.00	29.29
Torreon		Sp. quintal			
Middling, 15/16".........	"	101.4 lbs.	Peso	241.00	27.47
Houston-Galveston-New					
Orleans av. Mid. 15/16"..	"	Pound	Cent	XXXXX	32.20

Quotations of foreign markets reported by cable from U.S. Foreign Service posts abroad. U.S. quotations from designated spot markets.

1/ Nominal — ceiling prices.

Lightning Source UK Ltd.
Milton Keynes UK
UKHW041152150219
337137UK00013B/1570/P